ON POETRY STREET

Poems to share from
Scallywag Press

BRIAN MOSES

ON POETRY STREET

ILLUSTRATED BY
MARK ELVINS

Scallywag Press Ltd
LONDON

First published in 2024
by Scallywag Press Ltd
10 Sutherland Row
London, SW1V 4JT

Designed and typeset by Louise Millar

Printed and bound in China
by C&C Offset Printing Co. Ltd

001

British Library Cataloguing in Publication Data available

ISBN 978-1-915252-58-6

Contents

Welcome to Poetry Street

So, you want to write poetry . . .

First of all, let's try this simple test:

- Do you like stringing words together to see what they look like and what they sound like?
- Do you have rhythms dancing in your head as you drift through the day?
- Do you get told that you're a dreamer and that you should keep your feet on the ground?
- Do you find yourself bursting with creative ideas when you're in the supermarket, standing in a bus queue or trying to get to sleep at night?
- Do you rhyme all the time while your feet tap a beat?

If you answered YES to all or most of these questions then you're pretty much hooked on words.

On Poetry Street contains 52 poems, one for any week of the year, which can all serve as springboards to writing your own poetry.

Now – together – let's take a walk down Poetry Street!

On Poetry Street

See me walking down Poetry Street,
watch the way I tap my feet,
keeping time to an intricate beat
on Poetry Street.

My talent is here for all to see,
a star in the making – that's me!
hear my words, how they tumble free
on Poetry Street.

My poetic stanzas are tidy and neat,
my similes, surprising and sweet –
So many poets I might just meet
on Poetry Street.

See me rip my words from the page,
perform my poems on any stage,
watch me rap and roar with rage
on Poetry Street.

I'm raising the poetry decibel
with words that ring, clear as a bell,
so everyone who hears can tell
they're on Poetry Street.

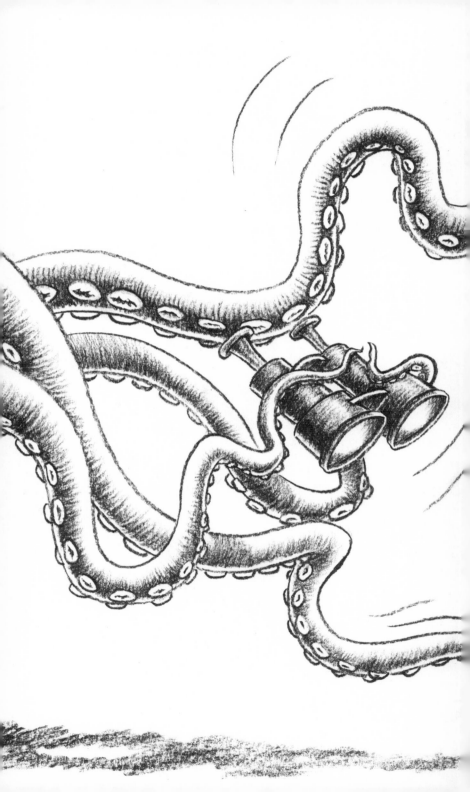

Always Wanted...

Always wanted
to sail round the world single handed,
to drive across the Sahara in a jeep,
to surf the giant waves at Malibu.

Always wanted
to race the bulls in Pamplona,
to hack my way though unexplored jungles,
to fight against the ocean around Cape Horn.

Always wanted
to slip past the tentacles of a giant squid,
to tiptoe round a sleepy lion,
to hug and be hugged by mountain gorillas.

Always wanted
to ride a raft through the waters of Grand Canyon,
to stand on the rim of a bubbling volcano,
to be a stowaway on a submarine.

Always wanted . . . and envious of those who have.

Safer Than . . . ?

Safer than asking King Kong for a date.
Safer than jumping from the Empire State.

Safer than skipping through fields of nettles
safer than playing catch with hot kettles.

Safer than skinny dipping in lava,
safer than chasing komodos in Java.

Safer than flying through a meteor shower
safer than climbing the Eiffel Tower.

Safer than surfing with an angry shark,
safer than finding a dragon in the park.

Safer than cosying up to a skunk,
safer than locking yourself in a trunk.

Much safer . . . !

Better than . . . !

Better than a slap round the face
with a wet fish.

Better than a dig in the ribs
from a rhino's horn.

Better than a clip round the ear
from a low flying seagull.

Better than a smack in the eye
from a turbo charged fly.

Better than a bash in the belly
from a honey seeking bear.

Better than a blow on the back of the legs
from an axolotl on full throttle.

Much better!

Villages

If I lived in the village of **Heart's Delight**
would every wish that I had come true,
would I find fulfilment in all that I do?

If I lived in the village of **Little Snoring**
would I find myself dreaming my life away
unable to wake at the start of the day?

If I lived in the village labelled **Dull**
would I live my life in black and white,
would the weather be cloudy and never bright?

If I lived in the village of **Grouse Hill**
would nothing ever be right for me,
would I be complaining constantly?

If I lived in the village of **Soar**
would I find my wings and take to the sky,
would birds admire my skill as I fly?

If I lived in the village that's called **Farewell**
would I always be leaving and never stay,
would 'Goodbye' be spoken every day?

But if I lived in the village of **World's End**,
I'd be careful, very careful indeed.

An Unlikely Alphabet
Of Animals In Even
Unlikelier Places

Aylesbury is the area for **aardvarks**
and **Bellingham** is brimming with **bees**.
In **Carlisle** you'll come across **caterpillars**
and in **Dover** you'll discover **donkeys**.
In **Egham**, **elephants** are everywhere
while in **Frome** all you'll find are **frogs**.
Grimsby is great for **goats**
and **Hastings** is home to **hot dogs**!
On the **Isle of Islay** I spied **iguanas**
and in **Jarrow** I juggled with **jellyfish**.
In **Kirklees** I was kind to **koalas**
but **llamas** in **London** were loutish.
Meercats have moved into **Margate**
and **Newbury** is well known for **newts**.

Orangutangs are oafish in **Oxford**
and **penguins** in **Penge** wear playsuits.
Quetzels are quiet in **Queenborough**
but **rhinos** are roaring in **Rochdale**.
Squirrels surf in the sea off **St. Ives**
while **turtles** in **Taunton** tell tales.
Umbrella birds unwind in **Ullapool**
while **vipers** are venomous in **Villiaze**.
Wildebeests wait in **Warrington**
for **X-ray fish** xeroxing **x-rays**.
Yaks yawn in **Yarmouth** and long for their beds
and all you get from **zebras** in **Zennor** are zzzzzs.

Holiday Advertisement

A holiday Beside the C Side
would be a great Delight,
Exceptional Fun in a Grand Hotel –
an Itinerary full of Joy bringing
a Kaleidoscope of Lovely Memories.
Nothing Off-Putting or Quirky,
Rather a Selection of Tempting
and Uplifting Vistas like a Wonderful
Xmas all Year and peaceful ZZZs
guaranteed each night.

Disguises

I disguised myself as a catapult
but all of my shots misfired.

I disguised myself as a ghost
but everybody saw through me.

I disguised myself as a high flying bird
but my wings were easily broken.

I disguised myself as music
but the notes I played were wrong.

I disguised myself as treasure
but nobody valued me enough.

I disguised myself as falling snow
and muffled myself in silence.

In the Land of Yesterday

In the Land of Yesterday,
my cat didn't bite me.
I didn't pick a fight with the boy next door.

In the Land of Yesterday,
my insult remains unspoken,
still locked away in my head.

In the Land of Yesterday,
my knee isn't cut,
my maths test remains unmarked,
and that short cut I took
for a dare – guess what –
I didn't go there.

And today I wouldn't have a care,
if I could have found a way to stay
safe in the Land of Yesterday.

In the Land of Do What I Want

In the Land of Do What I Want,
I'd squeeze more hours from the day
when it's Christmas,
when it's my birthday.

I'd never mind my manners
or make my bed,
or tidy up,
or make way for others.

In the Land of Do What I Want,
No one will remind me
to clean my teeth
or wash behind my ears.

No one will say, 'Don't do it,
it's dangerous.'

No one will mind if
I stay up late,
spend all day sleeping,
feed food I don't want to eat
to the drooling dog at my feet.

In the Land of Do What I Want,
I'll do what I want to all day long,
and nothing I do
will be wrong.

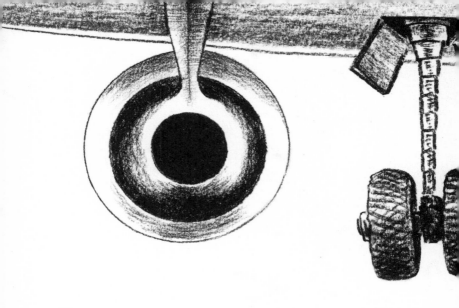

If My Whole Life Flashed Before Me

If my whole life flashed before me
I wouldn't want to remember:
the time I threw an apple through my neighbour's window,
the day my dad took his trousers off in public
    because a wasp had got inside them,
the moment I took hold of someone's hand in
      the supermarket
    and it wasn't Mum's,
the journey when we found ourselves driving along
    an airport runway,
the meal when I spilt red wine all over Dad's important
      business client,
and – worst of all
the kiss from Great Aunt Mabel when she forgot
    to put her teeth in.

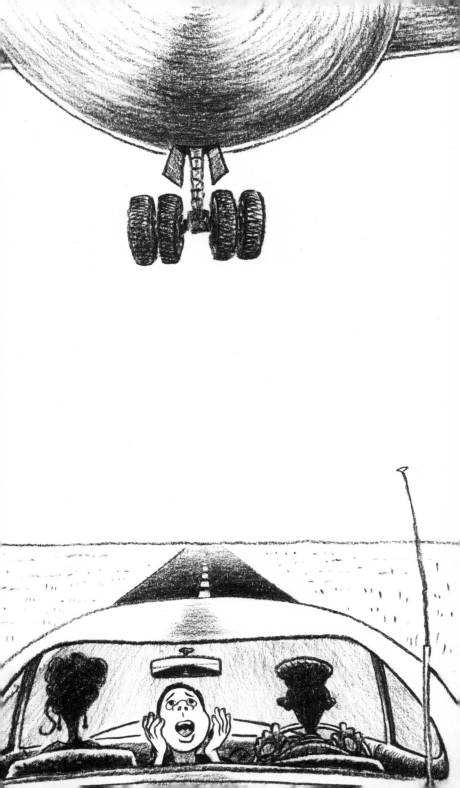

This Car

This car has been driven into walls and into sunsets.
It has slipped down mountain tracks,
almost ending up on its back.
This car has bumped and jolted over fields,
it has heard its own tyres squeal
to negotiate hairpin bends.
This car has almost drowned
in car washes and cloudbursts.
It has clowned around on the road
with crazy young hands at the wheel.
This car has been fingered by thieves
and abused by careless road users.
It has been seen at the scene of crimes.
This car heard a proposal of marriage
offered and then accepted.
This car once taxied its way round town,
trekked the motorway network,
rattled noisily through France.
This car, that once was mine,
that died on me,
is now badly beaten and scarred,
down at the breaker's yard.

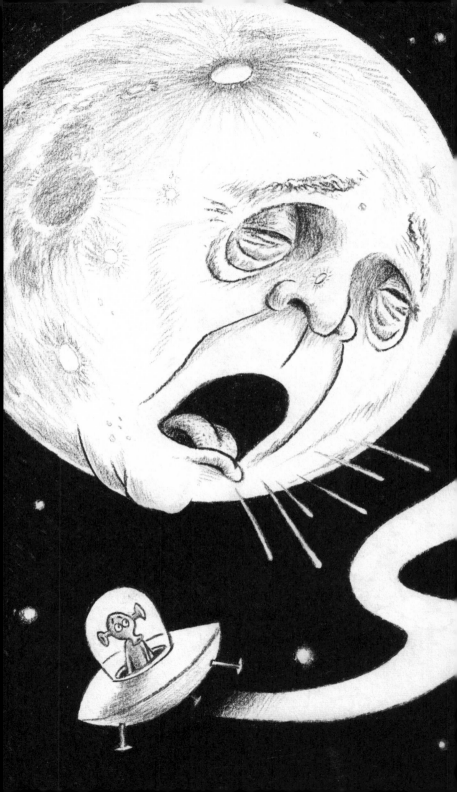

Still To Do . . .

Still not painted a new Mona Lisa.
Still not straightened the Leaning Tower of Pisa.

Still haven't taught the Moon how to sneeze.
Still not run a race on my knees.

Still haven't learnt to dance with a flea.
Still haven't identified every species of tree.

Still not built an ark like Noah.
Still not trained as an Olympic rower.

Still haven't fallen from the saddle of a horse.
Still haven't holed in one on a golf course.

Still haven't partied with aliens on Mars.
Still haven't found a pathway to the stars.

Still not come across a rainbow's pot of gold.
Still not discovered a cure for growing old . . .

But hoping, one day, that I will.

In the Hollywood Lost Property Box

In the Hollywood Lost Property Box
are . . .

Superman's tights, Dorothy's red shoes,
Mary Poppins' umbrella and one of Jaws' lost teeth.

E.T.'s borrowed bicycle, Luke Skywalker's light sabre,
Cruella de Vil's wig and a ticking clock
(inside a crocodile).

Lassie's collar, Zorro's mask,
Indiana Jones' hat and one of Robin Hood's arrows.

Frankenstein's bolt, Peter Parker's spectacles,
Lone Ranger's saddle and the key to Batman's batmobile.

Tarzan's loincloth, Cinderella's glass slipper,
Dracula's fangs and a Caribbean pirate's cutlass.

Please call and collect,
or any items remaining at the end of the day
will be given away
to charity shops in L.A.

Be . . .

Be ahead of the pack,
be a blur on the track.
Be a lion on the loose,
be a charging bull moose.
Be muscles of steel,
be a legend who's real.
Be a turbo charged cheetah,
be a swift record beater.

Be a fast flowing river,
be the urge to deliver.
Be a hawk in the sky,
   be a glint in an eye.
Be the push of a pedal,
be a shiny gold medal.

Dragon

Be a fiery roar,
be a guardian of treasure.
Be a flame in the night,
be a knight's worst foe.
Be a creature to fear,
be a symbol of danger.
Be the beating of wings,
be an evil hunter.
Be a shadow on the sun,
be a slashing claw.
Be a forest's secret,
be a nightmare,
suddenly there.

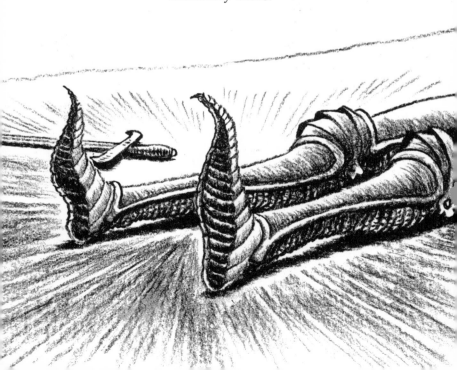

A Mouthful of Words

There are so many words that I like to say,
words like falafel and soubriquet,
mellifluous and didgeridoo,
winnebago, kalamazoo . . .

There are words that slide off the tongue,
words like slippery & slithery,
slimy, sloppy, slosh,
serendipity.

There are words that are trapped by teeth,
that are difficult to say –
anemone and discombobulate,
crepuscular, communiqué.

There are words that roll around in the mouth,
words like ululation,
desolation, isolation,
perambulation.

And I can't say 'higgledy-piggledy'
without laughing.

A Difficult Poem to Read Unless You've Swallowed a Dictionary

Regalia, Westphalia, saturnalia, paraphernalia.

Potato, tomato, tornado, lumbago.

Technology, tautology, chronology, archaeology.

Vernacular, oracular, spectacular, irregular.

Fascinated, anticipated, assassinated, disintegrated.

Now go find words from the dictionary
and string them together just like me.

Let the words tumble, feel them flow,
but is it a poem? Well, who knows?

My Wild and Crazy Side

I need to embrace
my wild and crazy side,
to do what I've always said I'd do . . .

Sail the ocean in a small canoe.
Ride on a train to Kalamazoo.
Teach swear words to a cockatoo.
Learn to play the didgeridoo.
Live in the mountains of Peru.
Yell loudly at midnight 'COCK A DOODLE DO'.
Leap on the back of a caribou.
Persuade an owl to play peekaboo.
Understand the language of emu.
Become a virtuoso on the kazoo.
Install central heating in an Inuit's igloo.
Invite a dragon to a barbecue.
Find a lucky golden horseshoe.
Master the flick of a cowboy's lasso.

I need to embrace
my wild and crazy side.

Don't you?

Reasons Why I Don't Play Air Guitar Anymore

1. My best friend borrowed it and never gave it back.

2. I left it on a train and now British Rail claim they can't find it.

3. My Dad said it made too much noise and confiscated it till I learn to play properly. (But how can I learn to play properly if I can't practise?)

4. I lost the instruction manual.

5. Mum said she thought it was broken and put it out for the bin men.

6. Every time I played it my dog started howling.

7. Dad sat on it and now the neck's broken.

8. Every time I picked it up I got an electric shock.

9. It produced such terrible feedback.

10. It needs new strings.

(Anyway, everyone plays air guitar these days – I've just ordered an air keyboard – from eBay of course!)

New Year Resolutions

1. I will never go hang gliding over
    active volcanoes.

2. I will always hate broccoli.

3. I will never shoot an albatross in
    Trafalgar Square.

4. I will not stop singing in the shower.

5. I will always enjoy eating chips.

6. I will never stand in the way of an
    angry bull.

7. I will always love my dog.

8. I will never tumble in a barrel over
    Niagara Falls.

9. I won't pick a fight with a boxing kangaroo.

10. I will never write another New Year's
    resolution that I can't keep.

To Do List

Swim the English Channel,
Ride a spitting camel,
Talk about enamel,
boringly.

Piggy back a teacher,
Find an extinct creature,
Interrupt a preacher,
noisily.

Learn to spin a plate,
Love someone I hate,
Predict my future fate,
worryingly.

Whisper to a whale,
Hike a black bear trail,
Pull a tiger's tail,
cautiously.

Be taught to train a flea,
Sail from sea to sea,
Climb a redwood tree,
skilfully.

Win Olympic Gold,
Survive the Arctic cold,
Grow young instead of old,
surprisingly.

Learn to dance the Twist,
Remember those I've kissed (ugh!)
Write another list,
(And another, and another . . .)
endlessly.

54

Omens

I saw the wild garlic flattened,
I saw the rain-drenched bee.
I saw the flecks of violet
in a bent wisteria tree.

I heard the babble of rooks,
I heard the startled horse.
I heard the river whisper
as the rocks broke up its force.

And I knew, for sure, that this year,
summer would be short.

Tired

I might get tired
of living in the same old place.

I might get tired
of hearing about the things
they do in space.

I might get tired
of zapping aliens when playing
computer games.

I might get tired
of watching fireworks as they quickly
burn up in flames.

I might get tired
of having the same friends calling round for tea.

But I know whatever happens
I'll never get tired of *me*
(or mushy peas or ribbons of cheese . . .)

So Bored

So bored,
I counted all the bricks
in the garden wall.
I talked to my dad
about his varieties of roses.
I watched our tortoise
make slow and steady progress
back to our vegetable patch.

So bored,
I stared out the window
watching the clouds drift by.
I rearranged all the socks
in my drawer.
I talked to my grandma
about her knitting.

So bored,
I even found my homework
interesting.
I even offered to
clean out the rabbit.
(What was I thinking . . . ?)

So bored,
so impatient,
so keen for the day to be over.

The day before my birthday
seemed endless.

Microscopic

If I were microscopic,
I could enter houses through keyholes,
I could live on the bridge of someone's nose
till a sneeze catapulted me off.

If I were microscopic,
I could travel through town in a dog's fur,
I could fly on the breeze as a speck of dust,
I could lodge in someone's eye,

If I were microscopic,
I could be head and shoulders above the crowd
as dandruff in uncared for hair,
I could rest on the wings of a fly on the wall
while listening to secrets being spoken.

If I were microscopic
I could ride on the back of an ant,
I could balance on the point of a pin,
I could hide behind a full stop.

If I were microscopic . . .

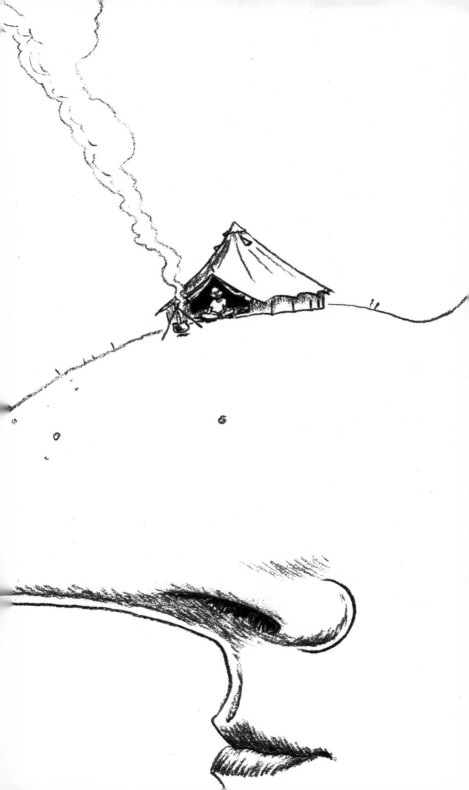

Always

Always the one who falls over,
always the one who grazes his knee,
always the one who speaks out of turn,
that's me.

Always the one who forgets,
always the one who embarrasses himself,
always the one who makes the wrong choices,
that's me.

Always the last to realise,
always the last to arrive,
always the last to stop talking,
that's me.

Always the one who goes the wrong way,
always the one who sings out of tune,
always the one who's seen and not heard,
that's me.

Worst Kisses

A fishy kiss from a mermaid
as you try to escape her embrace.

A chocolatey kiss from little sis
leaving brown stains on your face.

A silent kiss from a vampire
as he readies you for a feast.

A soppy kiss from big brother
saying sorry for being a beast.

A hissy kiss from a snake
as he wraps himself around you.

A slimy kiss from an ogre
leaving you covered in goo.

A seismic whiff of garlic
in a kiss from Auntie Joan.

An unfortunate kiss from Medusa
that quickly turns you to stone.

A sneaky kiss between Dad and Mum
as you do your best not to look.

And the longest kiss ever - 58 hours,
according to the Record Book.

The Elephant in the Room

Can't remember
when I first began to notice
there was an elephant in the room.

Maybe it's always been there.
Maybe it was hiding behind the settee
or tucked away inside a cupboard.

It was footprints across the room
that first alerted me,
mostly early morning
as it must have been active at night.

Then I woke once
and heard thumping.
It must have been bumping into furniture
but when I looked
it was always hiding.

I made phone calls,
spoke to zoos, wildlife parks –
but their elephants were all accounted for.
Elephants, it seems, do not go missing
very often.

Then, once, I was backing into the room
and the elephant was backing out.
We collided, bottom to bottom.

I said he could stay.
invested in an elephant size cat litter tray.
But he has no need,
I've never seen him feed.

We co-exist now, side by side.
He has his favourite TV programmes,
I have mine.

An elephant in the room need not be
a cause of strife.
My advice would be, if you find one,
welcome him into your life.

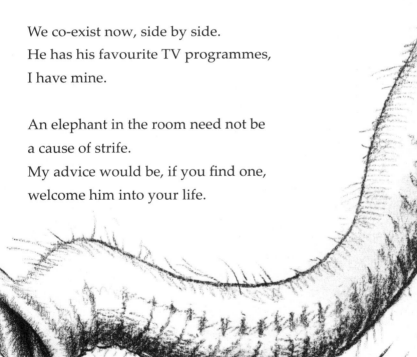

I Let the Cat Out of the Bag

Sometime between home & visiting the vets
I let the cat out of the bag.

He was, of course, spitting mad
that I'd bagged him
in the first place.

There was fury on his face.

He told me that he'd be finding
alternative accommodation,
a feeding station in another house
until he could bring himself
to forgive me.

It had been no fun
to be hustled and jostled and shaken about,
and even though he'd pleaded,
the most pitiful kind of miaows
had not succeeded in speeding
his release.

So he'd quietened, played dead,
and only then had I opened the bag
to check that the bundle of fur within
was still breathing.

An explosion of hissing, spitting cat
had shown me he was.

I tried everything to persuade him
back into the bag
but there wasn't a cat in hell's chance of that.

My hysterical cat is historical now,
lost, and still not found.

Painting the Town Red

I went out one night
to paint the town red.
No need for different colours,
let everything be red.

The parks, the streets, the buildings,
the underpasses and the alleyways,
I watched them all turn red.

I dipped my brush in the sunset,
saw paint dripping from traffic lights,
laughed as it smothered the green,
bringing traffic to a halt.

I saw it cover post boxes,
the odd remaining telephone box,
fire engines,
all redder than red now.

I loved painting the town red,
how it bled…

Till stumbling home,
thinking of other nights when I might
paint the town blue or green or brown,

I was caught
red-handed.

Grim

The railway's on strike,
someone's stolen my bike.

My coffee's gone cold,
the dog's getting old.

It's grim,
just grim.

The rain never stops,
the temperature drops.

The wifi's down,
I'm wearing a frown.

It's grim,
just grim.

My phone's up the creek,
the roof's sprung a leak.

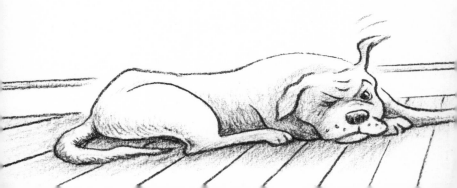

My car needs repair,
I'm losing my hair.

It's grim,
just grim.

As for lottery wins
my chances are slim
now everything's grim.

Just grim.

All Dogs Welcome

Fluffy dogs and toughie dogs.
Lonely dogs and homely dogs.
Crazy dogs and lazy dogs.
Grumpy dogs and lumpy dogs.
Dirty dogs and flirty dogs.
Happy dogs and snappy dogs.
Dozy dogs and cosy dogs.
Chewy dogs and skewy dogs.
Cranky dogs and manky dogs.
Gruffy dogs and wuffy dogs.
Growly dogs and prowly dogs.

All dogs welcome . . .

Even soggy dogs.

Not a Bad Morning for a Mutt

Had a run around with a Greyhound.

Had a chug through the mud with a Pug.

Ran from a tiff with a Bull Mastiff.

Had a brief canoodle with a Labradoodle.

Chose to scoot from a Malamute.

Raced through the rain with a huge Great Dane.

Had a jog with a Pyrenean Mountain dog.

Flew like an eagle when chasing a Beagle.

Avoided a fight with a West Highland White.

Went leaps and bounds with an Afghan Hound.

Found a real go-getter in a young Red Setter.

So thank you, guys,

it was really fun –

but you're all no-hopers

if you think you can outrun

ME!

What's Manky?

A banana skin trodden in,
an overflowing rubbish bin.

A kiss from your mum at the school gates,
unscraped, unwashed dinner plates.

Uncle Simon slurping soup,
a never cleaned out chicken coop.

Bubblegum attached to your shoe,
seagull poo on a seafront statue.

Mould growing on a slice of bread,
a slug infested flower bed.

And what's really manky,
a lace-edged, snot-filled hanky.

A Happy Poem

No room for doom or gloom,
this is a happy poem.

No time for whining or moaning,
no need for complaining,
this is a happy poem.

This poem will bring a smile to your face,
it's a poem just right for joy
or rejoicing.

It invites you to join in,
read along, clap your hands,
bang a drum.

It's a zing and zoom along kind of poem,
an always right, never wrong
kind of poem –

a Zip-A-Dee-Doo-Dah
sort of poem…

or it will be, now that I've finished it.

No Word of a Lie

My dad got baked into an apple pie,
when my train left the station, it started to fly.
It's really no word of a lie.

A see-saw flung me into the air,
I played chess with a polar bear,
I was frozen by a witch's stare.
It's really no word of a lie.

My sister heard a werewolf's cry,
my dog grew wings and took to the sky,
my cat played rugby and scored a try.
It's really no word of a lie.

I woke up this morning with purple hair,
I squeezed into a fox's lair.
It's really no word of a lie.

I found a fallen star still shining bright,
I flew away on the tail of a kite,
and this poem took all of two seconds to write.
It's really no word of a lie.

If I Could Travel Back in Time...

If I could travel back in time,

I'd ask the Romans how they got their roads
    so straight.
I'd ask the Vikings why they were filled with hate.

I'd ask King Henry why he needed several wives.
I'd ask a hangman, with hindsight, how he felt about
    ending lives.

I'd enquire of Queen Victoria why she always looked
    so sad.
I'd ask Guy Fawkes to consider if the plans he had
    were bad.

I'd ask the baker in Pudding Lane if he really set
    London alight.
I'd ask a wartime soldier what it felt like to go
    and fight.

The answers to all these questions, and many more,
    would be mine,
If only I could travel back in time.

Sleeping

I slept soundly beneath the stars
and slowly turned silver.

I slept peacefully by the sea
while waves of emotion flowed over me.

I slept lightly below moonbeams
and was touched by mystery.

I slept softly among clouds
and found myself floating away.

I slept deeply in a fishing boat
and reeled in my dreams all night long.

I slept fitfully among mountains
and woke to the wisdom of ages.

The North Face

This is the famous north face of our teacher
that's never been known to crack a smile.

This is the famous north face of our teacher,
few have scaled the heights to please her.

Some of us have tried and failed,
some of us knew we hadn't a hope,
some of us were brushed aside
or slid back down the slippery slope.

Not for her any creature comforts,
not for her any softening smile,
only the bleak and icy wastes,
of her glacial grimace.

This is the famous north face of our teacher,
all signs of weakness displease her.

But when our headteacher wanders in
and says what lovely work we've done,
there's a glimmer of something
that plays on her lips
like a hint of sun between mountains,
only to vanish again
when she starts to speak.

On a Day

On a day of disagreement,
I argued non-stop with myself.

On a day of ambition
I sought to climb mountains.

On a day of determination,
I worked at a maths problem till I solved it.

On a day of consternation,
all roads led me nowhere.

On a day of discontentment,
even the things that went right
didn't please me.

On a day of desperation,
I struggled to complete this poem.

Animal Antics

I've been beaten by a chihuahua
and mugged by a polar bear.
I've been piggybacked by a sloth
and transfixed by a lion's stare.

I've boogied and bopped with a budgie
and been pecked at by angry emu.
I've been bitten by a bison
and charged by a caribou.

I've been rattled by a rattlesnake
and jumped on by a frog.
I've been friendly with a fish
and partied with a pop star's dog.

I've been licked by the tongue of a llama
and hugged by a friendly gnu.
I've been badgered by a badger
and kicked by a kangaroo.

Now how about you?

Dear Bro

Scrolling down from
the hair on my head
to the soles of my feet,
I need to make it clear
that every part of me hates you.

There's no part of me
that would ever (billion years ever)
be mates with you.

The breath in my body
hates you.
Certainly the look in my eyes
hates you
and the words in my mouth
fall over each other in their eagerness
to tell you how much
I hate you.

I hate you enough
to drown you in a vat of perfume,
to flick you into the web
of a giant spider,
to arrange a blind date for you
with Medusa.

I hate you...

like the Sheriff of Nottingham
hated Robin Hood,
like Tom hates Jerry,
like our dad hates Arsenal.

Even my dreams hate you
and my best nightmares
find the worst fates for you.

And if you tease me again,
if you fail to please me
by spending all day
away from my sight,
you couldn't ever imagine
the horrors that I will unleash on you.

So be warned, be wise,
I'm closing my eyes now
and when I open them
I expect to see you gone.

But what's that in your hand?
You've bought me chocolate
and I hear the word 'Sorry'.

Forget what I said, big bro –
for a brother, you're the best!

Your loving Sis,
Juliet.

Questions About Slowworms

Is a slowworm slow
or can he be fast?
On sports days would he
always come last?
Is a slowworm too slow
to meet a mate?
Does he always turn up
late for a date?
I wonder how you tell
a boy from a girl?
When he falls in love
is his head in a whirl?
Does he hear love songs
and feel heartache?
Does he ever wish
he were really a snake?
Does he envy the glow
that a glowworm makes?
Does he have regrets?
Does he make mistakes?
Or is he content
with a warm sunny place?
Is that a smile we can see
on his face?

Mistakes

An ant's mistake
was to hide under somebody's shoe.

A sloth's mistake
was to post an entry form for the London Marathon.

A worm's mistake
was to stick his head above ground when a blackbird
was hunting.

A burglar's mistake
was to break into a police station.

A dragon's mistake
was to meet someone with a fire extinguisher.

A unicorn's mistake
was a failure to apply the brakes
when sliding down rainbows.

A slowworm's mistake
was to find a new home in a chicken run.

A teacher's mistake
was to get out of bed on a Monday morning.

Mistakes – I've made a few.
Have you?

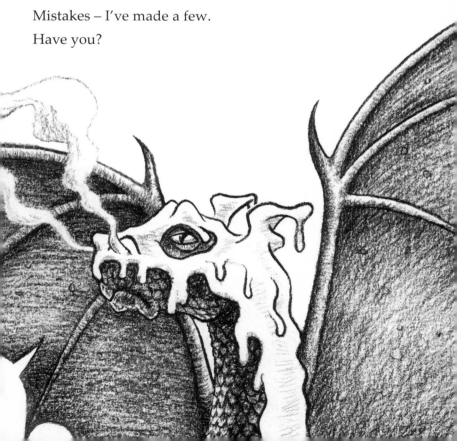

In Any City

There was one who did a dance,
a shuffle of feet across the sidewalk.
There was one with a sign –
'I hate to ask, you hate to give.'
There was one who played drums,
a symphony on saucepans and tins,
while another growled out
'Jumping Jack Flash'
as he strummed a banjo.
There was one humming endlessly,
some sort of mantra.
There was one in a doorway
tented by cardboard.
There was one sifting through debris
with his feet,

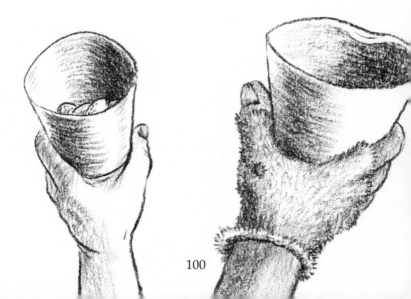

while another tenderly lifted cold pizza
from a waste bin.
There was one performing magic tricks
and another arguing with himself.
There was one asking the time
as if time really mattered.
There was one with another sign,
'Why lie – I could use a beer
and a burger.'
There was one, there were many,
each with his own Starbucks cup,
hopelessly, hopefully,
looking up at us
looking down.

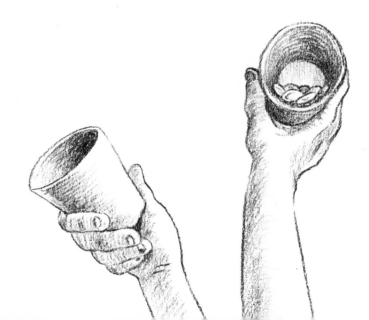

Travelling Shoes

I've got travelling shoes.

Shoes that take me from A to B,
sometimes by way of C.

Shoes that keep me connected,
one place leading to another.

Shoes that ramble, shoes that march.

Shoes that sometimes set off on their own
but always return to find me.

Shoes that take me back
to places I left behind.

Shoes that dawdle,
knowing how unwilling I am
to travel somewhere.

Shoes that escape
till I tie their laces together.

Shoes that control me,
save me from falling.

Shoes that sometimes tie me down,
keep me rooted, refuse to move.

Shoes with moods,
shoes with attitude.

Cool dude shoes.

Noble shoes
that treat my feet royally.
Shoes that flatter my feet.

Every sort of shoe.

But best are the shoes
from charity shops
where I walk in the footsteps
of others,

hearing stories along the way
of someone else's history.

If I had Ears the Size
of Satellite Dishes . . .

If I had ears the size of satellite dishes . . .

I could hear the buzz and whine of saws
as they toppled rainforest trees.

I could hear the soft beating
of a butterfly's wings.

I could hear a ladybird's footsteps on a leaf
and the arguments of ants under the ground.

I could hear mice scampering through
    the King's cellars
and a dog barking in New York.

I could hear the hum of alien messages zinging
    through space
and the breathing of an octopus beneath the sea.

But even with ears the size of satellite dishes,
I still wouldn't hear my mum telling me . . .

        to tidy my room!

I'd Rather Be Doing Anything Today Than Going to School

I'd rather tightrope walk across Grand Canyon or
    tumble over Niagara Falls in a barrel.

I'd rather have my feet nibbled by piranhas or try to
    tiptoe past a sleepy lion.

I'd rather eat brussels sprouts for my birthday tea or
    bungee jump from the Empire State Building.

I'd rather wander through the town in my pyjamas
    or practise juggling with dynamite.

I'd rather kiss a pot bellied pig or sleep in a nest
    of vipers.

I'd rather walk through a haunted forest at night
    or be invited to tea at Dracula's Castle.

I'd rather have a spitting contest with a camel
    or be forced to eat sardine sandwiches.

Yes, I'd rather be doing anything today
    than going to school...
Because school's just not cool enough for me.

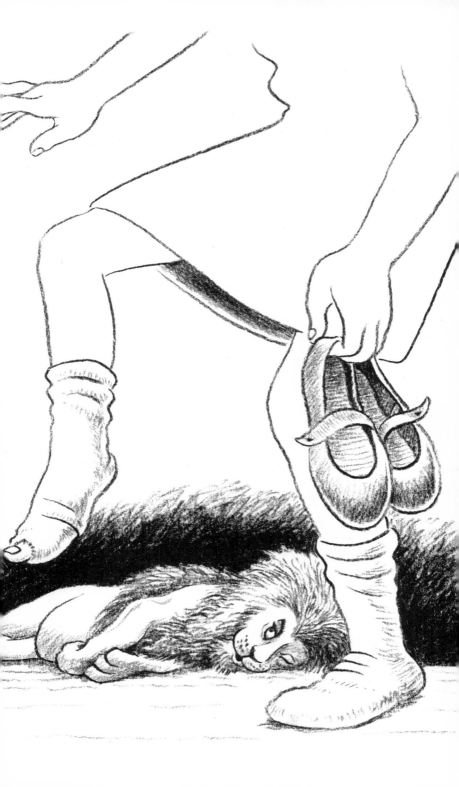

Can't

My mother used to say,
take the 't' out of 'can't' and you 'can'.
Or sometimes she'd say,
'There's no such word as can't.'
But I've found things I can't do . . .

I can't lick my nose with my tongue,
I can't bite my toenails,
I can't give the kiss of life to a dead beetle,
I can't scratch my ear with my foot
like my dog can,
I can't keep money in my piggy bank
without spending it,
I can't do the splits like my sister can,
I can't predict
    what my football team will do at the weekend.
(They sometimes surprise me, mostly dismay me!)

Take the 't' out of 'can't' and you 'can',
my mother said.
But I've got news for her:
however hard I try,
however hard I want to believe her,
there are still some things I just can't do.

New Superheroes

There are superheroes I never knew existed
in the pages of my local ad magazine.

Heroes who have overcome
the ordinariness of their occupations
to organise and surprise us.

I'm a big fan of
Upholstery Man
and the speed at which he'll repair
every tear.

Garage Door Man
will soon pay a call
and single-handedly lift
your fallen door.

If you need something shifted
from place to place,
Haulage Man will make it a race.

And Pond Man is the hero for you
when algae in your pond turns blue.

Then there's
Skip Man, Boiler Man, Septic Tank Man,
Driver Man, Digger Man, Tree Man,

And my favourites, that dynamic duo,
Tarmac Adam and
William the Concreter.

I'd Like To...

I'd like to fly south with the birds and winter in warmer places.
I'd like to be able to change the expressions on people's faces.

I'd like to travel America in a Wild West covered wagon.
I'd like to go questing with knights of old,
in search of a feisty dragon.

I'd like to invite a tree to accompany me on a walk.
I'd like to spend some time teaching small dogs how to talk.

I'd like to discover treasure in a chest beneath my bed.
I'd like to capture and tame all the scary thoughts in my head.

I'd like to tickle a trout and hope to hear it giggle.
I'd like to invent a new alphabet where every letter's a squiggle.

I'd like to shake the dust out of my deepest dreams.
I'd like to see the world where nothing is ever as it seems.

Exploring ideas on Poetry Street

There are fifty-two poems in this book, an idea for each week of the year. These poems are models for writing and can serve as frameworks on which you can hang your own ideas. But don't just follow the book from beginning to end, dip into it, see which ideas appeal, which ones jump out at you and make you think that you could write something like that. Also, don't be afraid to depart from the framework and initiate new patterns for your poems too.

Some of the poems make use of rhyme for the poem's rhythm. An effective rhyming poem can chime and ring as the words work together in surprising ways. Remember though that a weak rhyme can spoil the poem, so it is worth searching for the best possible one. You may find that you need to change the whole line around before you find a rhyme that works.

If you are really stuck for a rhyme, try using a rhyming dictionary. It will give you a list of rhymes that you probably haven't thought of yourself.

There are, of course, various ways of rhyming. Some of the poems in this book are written in rhyming couplets where pairs of lines have the same rhyme. Examples of these are 'Still to Do' (p. 35), 'Grim' (p. 72) and 'If I Could Travel Back in Time' (p. 84).

In 'Animal Antics' (p. 93) the second and fourth lines rhyme in each verse.

Others, such as 'To Do List' (p. 52), have three lines that rhyme, or four lines as with 'On Poetry Street' (p. 10) while the poem 'My Wild and Crazy Side' (p. 46) keeps the same rhyme all through the poem.

The poems 'Be' (p. 38) and 'Dragon' (p. 40) show two contrasting ways of writing a poem. 'Be' is a rhyming poem, but 'Dragon' doesn't rhyme. It relies on the repetition of the word 'Be' to give it a rhythm.

Other poems that rely on repetition to help give them their rhythm are, 'Better Than' (p. 16) and 'This Car' (p. 32) where one line begins with – 'This car . . .' and the next with 'It . . .'. You could try other subjects such as This Dog, This Library Book, This Pen, This Football.

Some of the poems in the book are what I call 'List poems'. Some people might say that poems like 'A Difficult Poem to Read Unless You've Swallowed a Dictionary' (p. 44) or 'Reasons Why I don't Play Air Guitar Anymore' (p. 48) are not really poems at all, but as a poet I have poetic licence, and what's the point of having it if I don't make use of it occasionally!

Other possible topics for writing list poems could be – reasons why my train was late this morning, reasons why I keep being late for school (but not the cliché – the dog ate my homework!). Reasons why each goal wasn't a goal in our school team's disastrous football match, reasons why I always manage to avoid washing the dishes, and so on.

Similarly with 'In the Hollywood Lost Property Box' (p. 36) you can think about what might be found in other lost property boxes – a football stadium changing room, No 10 Downing Street, Buckingham Palace, a school staffroom or Jurassic Park.

Writing new year resolutions always sounds like a good idea, but if you're anything like me, you've broken them before you've even got through the first day of the new year. But . . . what if you could write new year resolutions that you could be 100% certain you could keep and never break? Take a look at 'New Year Resolutions' (p. 50) and write some of your own.

Another type of poem is one that I call a 'Research poem' where I need to browse the internet or a book or two before I've gathered enough material to write the poem. An example of this type of poem is 'Villages' (p. 18) where I needed an atlas and a list of villages with strange names.

For 'Not a Bad Morning for a Mutt' (p. 76) – I looked through a book of dog breeds, and for 'New Superheroes' (p. 110) I found all my material in a local ad mag.

And then there are the ones I call 'Overheard Poems'. 'Dear Bro' (in the form of a letter, p. 94) was inspired by hearing a young girl shout out to her older brother, 'Every part of me hates you!' Be alert for strange things people say and write them down. I find that they can often trigger poems.

The poems 'The Elephant in the Room' (p. 66), 'I Let the Cat Out of the Bag' (p .68) and 'Painting the Town Red' (p. 70) were the result of skimming through a dictionary of idioms. I would define an idiom as an expression that has a different meaning from its real one, and the English language is full of them: 'A red rag to a bull', 'Blow the cobwebs away', 'Down in the dumps' and 'Out of the ark' are other examples, any of which might inspire a poem.

In 'Questions About Slowworms' (p. 96), the questions reveal something about the creature – that he's slow, that he's not a snake and that he likes a warm sunny place. Other poems are about emotions – for example 'A Happy Poem' (p. 80) – and you could try writing about what's happy, embarrassing, boring, annoying, frightening or sad. What's sad? – a dog that needs a new home/ a broken garden gnome.

'The North Face' (p. 88) is an extended metaphor poem, which compares the harsh face of a strict teacher to the north face of a mountain where there is often very little sunlight. It then keeps the comparison going throughout the poem. Another example of this type of poem is 'The Sea' by James Reeves where he compares the sea to a hungry dog.

Remember too, that the two words, 'What if?' are the writer's best friends. 'What if My Whole Life Flashed Before Me?' (p. 30), 'What if I Had Ears the Size of Satellite Dishes?' (p. 104).

The last line of the last poem talks about seeing the world where nothing is ever as it seems. That's what I like to do, and if you choose to do that too, you'll be on Poetry Street.

B. M.

About the Poet

BRIAN MOSES had dreams, growing up, of becoming a musician. But it was Bob Dylan's lyrics that fired his teenage imagination. Then he encountered the 'Mersey Sound' poets and he was hooked. Starting out as a teacher, he wrote poems for his pupils and their response encouraged him to become a full-blown, published poet. Now, more than 200 books later – either as author or anthologist – he has sold over one million copies and has been labelled 'one of Britain's favourite children's poets' by the *National Poetry Archive*. Music, with its rhythm and repetition, informs much of his work and he performs poetry and percussion shows across the UK and abroad.

Brian lives in a small Sussex village with his wife, Anne, and their black Labrador, Jess. He says that his best ideas come to him when he is 'out walking the dog'.

About the Illustrator

MARK ELVINS abandoned his career in a Law Firm some years ago for the far less lucrative one of printmaking and illustration. He takes his inspiration for his printmaking from the countryside around him – the Lake District, Yorkshire and Scotland. His anarchic sense of humour comes to the fore in his children's book illustrations – as demonstrated right here, on Poetry Street. He has illustrated several fiction titles for Scallywag Press, including the Flyntock Bones trilogy, but this is the first time he has ventured into the realms of illustrating poetry.

Mark lives in Harrogate, Yorkshire with his wife, Leesa, and their French Bulldog, Peanut Bim (see p28!). When he is not at his desk drawing, or in the kitchen making cheese toasties, he is 'out walking the dog . . .'

About the Publisher

SCALLYWAG PRESS was founded in 2018, with the aim of publishing books that entertain and engage young readers. We love books where words and pictures both play their different parts to convey moments of drama, emotion and humour. We love books that reflect on our lives and provide valuable perspectives which could be useful to readers of any age. We love books as beautiful objects. *On Poetry Street* is Scallywag's first collaboration with Brian Moses. To find out more about his writing, school workshops and performances, visit www.brianmoses.co.uk